THE INDIANS
and the
CALIFORNIA MISSIONS

by
Linda Lyngheim

Illustrated by
Phyllis Garber

Langtry Publications

Van Nuys, California

To my parents who traveled with me along the coast of California to visit and explore all twenty-one missions.

(For book ordering information, please turn to last page)

Library of Congress Catalog No. 84-80543
ISBN: 0-915369-00-1

Copyright © 1984 by Linda Lyngheim

LANGTRY PUBLICATIONS
7838 Burnet Avenue
Van Nuys, CA 91405-1051

2   3   4   5   6   7   8   9   10

ACKNOWLEDGEMENTS

I want to thank the staff of the following libraries and organizations for their help in aiding my research of this book: the Glendale Public Library, the Pasadena Public Library, and the California Historical Society and library. A special thank you to Marilyn Ziebarth and Kirsten Elliott are due for their helpful comments on my manuscript.

FOREWORD

The California that is home to millions of people today started as the land of thousands of Indians of many languages. It is hard to imagine how it must have been. When you take a trip on the busy freeways and pass through its cities or by its farms, there are so many things that keep us from understanding how the state really started. If you keep your eyes open you may spot a beautiful old church building right in the middle of a busy city. Some of these old buildings were the beginning of the state the way we know it today.

In 1769, a small Spanish priest, crippled by a leg injury, walked into California at what is today San Diego. Here the story of modern California begins. Linda Lyngheim, the author of this book, takes you on a trip through the years of beginning. This book will help you understand the spirit and courage of Padre Serra, the man the state leaders called "the founder of California." His statue stands in the Capitol Building in Washington. In his hands he holds a small mission building. As you read this book, you will learn what these missions were and why they are still important today.

----Don Oliver
    Publisher, *California Weekly Explorer, Inc.*

PREFACE

It has been since the 1950's that anyone has published a book especially for children on the California missions. As a children's librarian for six out of my nine years as a librarian, I watched children struggling to read adult books on this subject.

Children, librarians, and teachers keep requesting books on this topic that fourth graders must study in California. It was through this need and my own interest in local history and writing that prompted me to author this book. I spent three years researching, writing, and visiting the missions to gather my information. My hope is that those who read it will find it useful in bringing alive this time in California history.

CONTENTS

THE INDIANS
and the
CALIFORNIA MISSIONS

California Missions

San Francisco Solano

San Rafael Arcangel

San Francisco de Asis

San Jose de Guadalupe

Santa Clara de Asis

Santa Cruz

San Juan Bautista

San Carlos Borromeo

Nuestra Senora de la Soledad

San Antonio de Padua

San Miguel Arcangel

San Luis Obispo de Tolosa

La Purisima Concepcion

Santa Ines

San Buenaventura

Santa Barbara

San Fernando Rey de Esp

San Gabriel Arcangel

San Juan Capistrano

San Luis Rey de Francia

San Diego de Alc

1
DISCOVERY OF CALIFORNIA

During the 16th Century, Spain and other European countries explored the world looking for new lands to own. At that time an explorer named Juan Cabrillo sailed from Spain and founded San Diego. He claimed the land for his country in the year 1542.

For a long time no one seemed interested in the faraway California. Russian fur trappers and traders sold many furs. They had a large trading post in Northern California. Spain thought Russia would take California away from them.

In 1769, King Charles III of Spain decided on a plan. He chose Jose de Galvez to be viceroy (vice-king) to govern

New Spain (Mexico). He would carry out the king's orders to send soldiers, explorers, and missionary padres to set up missions. There would be twenty-one missions built along the coast of California. Each would be spaced a day's walk from the next one.

Galvez chose Captain Don Gaspar de Portola to lead the military part of the expedition. Father Junipero Serra would be the church President, in charge of establishing the missions. Under this plan, the padres would interest the native Indians in becoming Christians. The Indians would help run the missions, taking them over in time.

Along with the missions, the Spaniards would build *presidos* or forts for soldiers to guard the land and people.

To Spain this was an easy way to claim California peacefully. More than two hundred years had passed since the Spaniards had been here. This time they came to settle California.

2

SPANISH SETTLEMENT

THE SPANIARDS RETURN

Father Serra excitedly thought of the days ahead. At last his dream would come true. The missions would soon be built. Tomorrow they would begin their long journey from Mexico to San Diego. Tonight he could not sleep. In the dim candlelight glow of his room, Father Serra walked the hours away until morning. A fearful question troubled his thoughts. Would the Indians come once the missions were built?

INDIANS WERE LIVING ON THE LAND

Most Indian tribes welcomed the Spaniards, including Chief Yanunali and his people. These easygoing, independent people had never seen a white man before. They asked many questions. Who were they? What did they want? Why were they on Indian land? Their clothing was strange. They acted odd to this Chumash tribe, as to other Indians.

The Spaniards whispered among themselves as they saw the Indians on the hillside. Carefully, the Indians came closer. First came the men who wore little or no clothing. The women followed closely behind dressed in deerskin skirts. Colorful paint and tattoos (marks on their skin) decorated their bodies.

Quickly, the Spaniards reached for the brightly-colored gifts they had brought with them. They offered these to the Indians as a sign of friendship. The excited Indians picked up the sparkling beads and fingered them in the sunlight. The Indians ran off but later came back with food for the tired, hungry strangers.

INDIAN VILLAGES

All California Indians lived simply in huts. This tribe lived in a usual village of 80 people. Their huts were made of tule grass.

Other tribes built houses of brush or bark. No one could understand their neighbors because California Indians spoke 135 dialects (different ways of saying the same language).

HUNTING FOR FOOD

The Indians spent much of their time looking for food since they did not plant crops. The men hunted with bows and arrows and trapped wild game. Those living near the ocean caught fish. Their meals included deer, fish, rabbit, bear, and mice. They ate more unusual food like grasshoppers, lizards, snakes, and worms.

Indians hunted for deer, rabbit, and bear

Those living near the ocean caught fish

Women dug in the ground for roots. They gathered seeds and picked berries from the bushes. When the food was gone, they moved on. The Indians took what the land had to offer them. Little went to waste.

At times they did not have enough to eat. Their way of life could be hard. Then the Spaniards came. They offered food, shelter, and religion to any Indians who wanted to change their religion to Christianity. Many chose this life.

3

LIFE AT THE MISSIONS

The Indians who chose Christianity came to live at the mission. They had to work hard to keep it going. They plowed the fields and worked in the workshops. They built buildings, hunted for food, and cared for livestock. The Indians ate the food they raised, wove the clothes they wore, and lived in the houses they built.

At the beginning, each mission was given the supplies it needed to start. Two padres served at each mission. One taught the Indians Christianity. The other showed them how to do the work. From that time on, everything depended on their success! They supported themselves.

BUILDING THE MISSION

Pounding, clanking, and chopping noises rang out as building began. Sweat dripped from the faces of the soldiers and Indians as they worked in the hot sun. Chief Yanuanli and his men came to help the white man build their buildings. First, they stomped and pounded the clay earth with their hands and feet to make adobe bricks. They added water and straw. They mixed it together and poured it into a mold. Out came an adobe brick 23 inches long, 11 inches wide, and 2-5 inches thick. The bricks were laid out in the sun to dry.

Other men gathered wood and built a blazing fire in the brick oven called a *kiln*. All day long they slid bricks in and out of the oven to bake. These bricks were harder. They lasted longer than the sun-dried adobes. But they took more trouble to make.

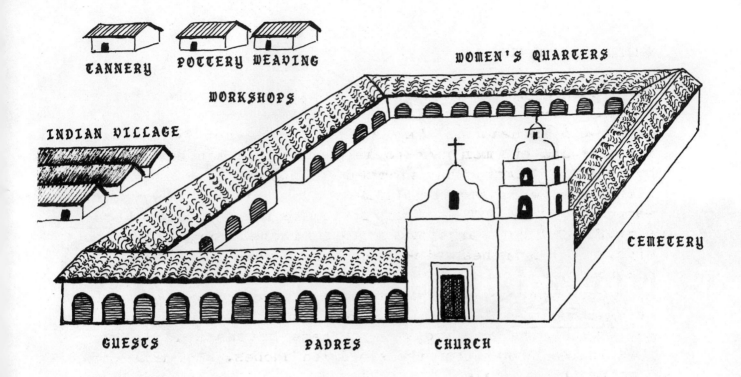

TANNERY   POTTERY WEAVING

WORKSHOPS

INDIAN VILLAGE

WOMEN'S QUARTERS

CEMETERY

GUESTS   PADRES   CHURCH

The Indians knew how to build simple grass huts. The padres wanted to build larger buildings out of adobe bricks for the mission. The Indians had never built houses like that before. Neither had the padres. The padres had to read books about building and design. From these they learned what to do. They drew up plans on paper to show the Indians.

The padre pointed to the drawing as he talked to the Chief. The church would go here, he explained. The padres' rooms, storehouses, housing for unmarried women, soldiers' barracks (rooms), and indoor workshops would all be built around a square. He pointed to a place outside the square as the Indians gathered around him. If they chose to live at the mission, they would build their huts or adobe houses here.

19

The Indians clapped one adobe brick on top of another, slapping mud in between. They built up the walls and piled straw on top for roofs. This is what they used for their own huts. But straw easily caught fire and burned up. Too many buildings burned along with them.

Later, tile roofs were used. They did not burn. The Indian women helped to get the clay earth ready. They mixed it with water. The men patted the wet clay on logs to shape them. They baked the wet tiles in the outdoor ovens until they were dry and hard.

The Indian man hit the shining axe blade against the tree. It sliced the bark. Blow by blow the crack widened and gave way. The tree crashed to the ground. The men took the saw and cut the wood into long planks to load in the cart.

The oxen pulled the heavy load back to the mission. Wood was used as beams to help hold up the adobe walls, ceilings, and roofs.

DAILY LIFE OF THE INDIANS

Ding-dong, ding-dong, ding-dong. The ringing of the bells told the Indians it was time to wake up.

Quickly, a young Indian boy pulled on his shirt and pants. He slid his feet into the smooth leather sandals his brother had made. Mateo, son of Chief Yanunali, did not want to be late for church.

He could hear the sounds of others stirring as the mission community came to life. Joining his friends, he crowded into the church. He took his place with the men and boys. Women and girls sat together on the other side. Then all was quiet.

The church service began. The padre came out dressed in white satin robes sewn with red and gold flowers. These clothes were different from the dull gray robes he usually wore. But church was an important event. The padre chanted. Soon music and singing filled the air. The Indians said their prayers.

After church, everyone sat down at long wooden tables. Women from the kitchen dished out steaming hot corn mush into wooden bowls. They ate their fill. Afterward, the padres told them what work to do for the day.

The Yanunali family went different ways. Mateo ran off with the younger children to learn Spanish and religious lessons from the padre.

At noon they all came together for lunch. The smell of
hot *pozole* (stew) filled the air. Mateo sat at the table
and spooned the tasty vegetables and beef down. After lunch
everyone took a rest, a *siesta*. Then they went back to work
for a few more hours.

In the late afternoon his parents visited with friends,
while he played with Francisco. They sat down to a dinner
of corn mush and bread. At the end of the day, the bells
rang calling the Indians to church.

WORK IN THE FIELDS

The hot sun shone down on the men in the fields as they hoed long rows of crops. Close by, a man guided the wooden plow as it dug into the rich, brown earth. Chief Yanunali was in charge of the workers in the field. He showed other men how to do the work. He watched as men followed behind the plow. They dropped seeds of corn, wheat, beans, peas, and barley into holes. They covered them up with earth. The men would water and care for the crops. They would grow into food for the people at the mission to eat.

Chief Yanunali and his wife Juana and children Mateo, Pablo, and Antonia Maria liked life at the mission. The padres were kind to them. He no longer was called chief. Now he was given the Christian name of Pedro.

He looked up and saw his brother herding sheep on the hilltop and waved. Juan waved back. Many Indians roamed the large mission lands looking after cattle, sheep, oxen, horses, and goats.

WORK IN THE WORKSHOPS

Workshops burst with noise and work. In the leather shop Pedro's oldest son Pablo cut, hammered, and sewed the leather into shoes. Blacksmiths, carpenters, tanners, and builders also worked at their trades.

Pablo making shoes for people

Blacksmith making horseshoes

Tanner stretching cattle hide

The click-clack of the wooden loom could be heard as
Juana, Pedro's wife, moved it back and forth. The loom was
built by Spanish carpenters. She was weaving rough blue
wool into cloth. Juana talked to other women as they comb-
ed, carded, and spun the wool into yarn. Some women dyed
the yarn. Others cut the cloth and sewed it into clothes.
Women made skirts, blouses, and pants for the Indians of the
mission. They also made robes for the padres. Weavers wove
blankets in bright colors. They were clever and skillful at
weaving.

In the kitchen Pedro's daughter, Antonia Maria, made corn mush for the evening meal. She took a large, flat stone and put corn on it. Then she picked up a smaller stone and used it to grind the corn.

Everyone worked hard for the mission community. On special days they visited their old villages. Mateo sometimes wished they could live there with their old friends. But the padres would not allow it.

VILLAGE LIFE BEFORE COMING TO THE MISSION

Mateo remembered village life before they moved to the mission. They had roamed the land. No one had told them what to do.

Medicine woman chasing "bad spirits" from a sick person

Their gods had been different. They had believed in the Sky Father and Earth Mother. All things in nature like trees and rivers were respected. They had good and bad "spirits" living in them. Mateo remembered how the medicine woman of their village had shaken her rattles to chase away the bad spirits. Once when he was sick, she had given him medicine from a plant to make him well. Some villages had medicine men, others medicine women. Their dances and songs had made the gods happy. They had not prayed to them like to the one God at the mission.

How many times had his father brought them to visit the mission? Many, Mateo thought. His father had talked to the padre about the new religion. The padre wanted them to come to live at the mission. When they decided to give up the old religion and believe in the new God, they had to move to the mission. They became Christians. Many from their tribe came with them. Others liked their old ways and stayed in the village.

Not everyone who came to the mission liked it. Their new life was so different from the old. Sometimes the hard work never seemed to end. The padres were always telling them what to do. There were Indians who missed village life. For these reasons, some of the Indians changed their minds. They wanted to leave the mission.

The padres would not let them. They believed once the Indians said they would become Christians, they could not change their minds. Many Indians ran away. The soldiers galloped after them on horses. They brought the runaways back and punished them. The Indians could not understand why they were treated so harshly. There were other Indians who liked the mission and wanted to stay.

GAMES AND PLAY

Mateo ran off to play. He met Francisco outside the church. The boys challenged each other to a foot race.

They ran as fast as they could until one touched the apple tree. Francisco won.

The boys fell down breathless and laughing on the ground. They turned to watch a game of tug-of-war. Boys and men on one side of the rope. Girls and women on the other. A rope stretched between them. They pulled the rope back and forth. Both sides pulled hard. Suddenly, the men gave a jerk. The women and girls fell over each other laughing. Mateo and Francisco roared with laughter.

In the late afternoon work was finished. Men, women, and children gathered in the courtyard to visit and play games. Younger children spun tops made from acorns. Many ball games like those we have today took place. Friends cheered them on. They played guessing games too.

Mateo liked *fiestas* (parties) best. On church holidays the mission rang with laughter and excited shouts. The Indians played more games. Bear and bullfights also took place. At night the square glowed with candles for dancing. Work was forgotten and left for another day.

THE SOUNDS OF MUSIC

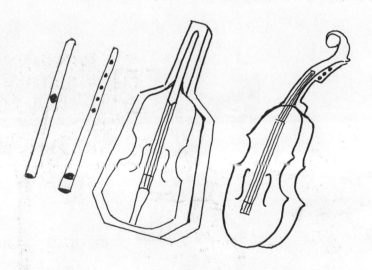

carved bone flute, five-stop flute, bass viol, violin

31

The sound of flutes filled the air. Pablo carved a flute for himself out of animal bone. He carved one for Mateo out of wood. The two sat happily in the late afternoon blowing on their instruments. They enjoyed music for as long as they could remember. Back in their village they had played flutes.

Now at the mission Pablo and his father sang and played in the church choir. What a great many instruments to choose from! Pablo plucked the strings of violins and guitars. He ran his fingers over the smooth shiny wood of harps, violas, and basses. He clanged and played cymbals, triangles, and drums. One of the padres helped Pablo make a violin since there were few of these. He hoped one day to play the barrel organ with its strange sounds.

The bells rang all day long. The Indians could tell by the bells when to go to church, to eat, and to work. Bells came in all sizes, shapes, and sounds. Some bells were large and heavy. The bell ringer who rang these had to move quickly away to not get hit.

THE ART OF THE INDIANS

An Indian dipped his brush into the red paint and care-fully stroked it on the church wall. Then he leaned back to look at his artwork. He added blue paint. He had mixed the paints from the flowers and plants he gathered. He squeezed the juice from a flower into the pot. Then he mixed it with olive oil. The bright designs made the plain adobe walls pretty.

Artists carved wood and stone statues. They made beau-tiful objects for the church and missions.

Down by the river, Mateo watched the women choose reeds
and brush. They used these to weave their baskets. Only
women were allowed to make the baskets. Like all California
Indians, they wove beautiful baskets with difficult designs.
They wove them in all sizes and shapes for their many uses.
Most were made in the shape of a bowl. They were made in
colors of yellow, brown, black, and white. Only black
needed to be dyed. They made it from a berry called elder-
berry. They used baskets to carry babies, hold food and
water. They even wore them for caps. Since they did not
have metal bowls, they used them for cooking.

Clay pots were made to keep things in. They used a
basket as a form to shape the clay. When the wet clay was
dry, they put it in the fire to bake. Women taught their
daughters and passed down the art of basketmaking. Though
the California Indians made little pottery or jewelry, they
were good basketmakers.

THE MISSIONS

(Each mission has its own story to tell. The story of
the missions is really the story of the people. It is about
the Indians and the padres who lived, struggled, and even
died out in the wild lands of early California.)

4

SAN DIEGO DE ALCALA

First Mission, founded July 16, 1769

The Indian children watched from the hills. Afraid, they crowded together to see what would happen. What a strange sight! Sheep and cattle and goats wandered along. They were followed by white men. The group stopped.

A short man who wore a gray robe stepped forward. He planted a wooden cross in the ground. He dropped to his knees. The others did the same. Singing filled the air. The ceremony ended with a great blast of noise! Gunfire from the soldiers' rifles. The Indians had never seen guns before.

The soldiers marched along the rough, dusty trail on foot. Father Serra limped on his hurt leg, caused by insect bites. The men arrived in San Diego tired and sick. Many needed rest and care.

The excitement of adventure caused others to go on. Captain Portola was in charge of the land expedition. He gathered up the healthy men and went to search for Monterey Bay.

Diegueno Indians living nearby came to visit the Mission. These visits were not friendly. The Indians did not like the Spaniards on their land. Neither the Indians nor the Spaniards could understand each other. They spoke different languages. The Indians wanted them to leave.

The expedition could not find Monterey Bay. The discouraged men came back to San Diego. They found many men were going hungry and others had died. The supply ship that was to bring food had never come. Portola insisted they must give up and go back to Mexico.

Father Serra pleaded with him. The Indians would never know Christianity if the missions were not founded. Finally, he talked Portola into waiting a few days. Surely the ship would come by then. But it did not. It was the last day before they were to go back. The white sails of a ship suddenly came into sight. Shouting and cheering broke out among the men. The ship, the *San Antonio*, had come in time.

The ship brought food and medicine and supplies. Captain Portola and his men started out again for Monterey. Father Serra wanted to go with them this time.

They left two padres and a group of soldiers behind to run the new Mission. They planted seeds for crops to feed the people. But the crops did not grow well. The land had too little water and poor soil. This made them move the Mission and build a new one a few miles away.

Not many Indians came. As time passed, the Indians became less friendly. Their leaders did not like the padres telling their people what to do. They did not want them to give up the old religion.

On the night of November 5, 1775, an angry band of Indians attacked the Mission. Fire blazed! Arrows and gunfire flew through the air.

Padre Luis Jayme rushed out to try to stop the Indians. "Love God, my children!" he shouted before he died.

The bows and arrows of the Indians were not as strong as the guns of the Spaniards. Many people were killed. Wounded from both sides lay bleeding. The Indians lost, but they brought those who were hurt to the Mission for help.

The Indians were friendlier to the white man after the battle. But not many were interested in living at the Mission.

The wheat swayed back and forth in the afternoon wind. Yellow cornstalks shot up to the blue sky. The new land was good for farming. Cattle grew fat on the green grass. This supplied the Mission with food and products. Trades were never good at this Mission.

What about the Indians? Would they always be unfriend- ly? Would they never know Christianity? Father Serra hoped not.

A young Indian boy visited often at the Mission. Father Serra taught him Spanish. He asked the boy to find an Indian couple who would be interested in having their child baptized. Baptism is a ceremony given for a person to become a Christian. Father Serra happily waited for the event. He dipped his hand in the baptismal bowl to sprinkle holy water on the baby's head. Suddenly, an Indian ran up and snatched the baby away from Father Serra. The Indian ran off with it. The baby was never baptized. This event saddened the padre.

Mexico became independent from Spain. The padres were told to leave the Mission. For years weeds grew on land no one cared for. Walls of buildings crumbled and fell. The government gave the Mission away to Santiago Arguello. They gave it to him for his good service to the government.

TODAY AT THE MISSION

Singing fills the old adobe church once more during church services. The church is small and plain inside. The padres who served the Mission are buried in the floor. This was a custom of early California.

Outside, the adobe building looks simple. The tall bell tower climbs to 46 feet high. Five bells hang inside. The largest one weighs over 1,000 pounds.

A walk in the garden will find a statue of Father Serra. He was the first President of the Missions. A large cross marks the spot where Father Jayme was killed in the Indian attack. The Indian graveyard nearby is the oldest one in California. It is here that the missions of California began. Mission San Diego is called the *Mother of the Missions* because it was the first.

5

SAN CARLOS BORROMEO (CARMEL)

Second Mission, founded June 3, 1770

The tall, green pine trees could be seen in the distance. The water of the bay was clear and blue. The men aboard the ship cheered! At last they had found Monterey Bay. They settled near its banks for a short time.

First, the men realized they must solve the problem of food. It took time to plant crops and for them to grow. Game ran wild on the new land. Why not go hunting? The men organized a hunting party. They headed for the Valley of the Bears. They returned leading mules loaded down with 6,000 pounds of bear meat for the Mission.

The following year, they moved the Mission to Carmel Valley. Here in the natural forest setting they did not have any of the troubles of the old land. There had been no water on the other land, and the soil had been poor. On the new land a river flowed with fresh water. The rich soil brought them good crops.

Father Serra chose this mission as his home when he was not off founding other missions. He learned the language of the Eslenes Indians who lived near the Mission. He hoped to tell them about Christianity. The Indians were friendly, and he hoped they would want to accept the new religion.

A stone craftsman from Mexico was sent for to design a new church. He hammered and carved the yellow stone, showing the Indians how to build the church. The finished church was grand! A window shaped in a star fit in the center. The rays of sunlight shone through it. The unusual style made it look different from any other mission church.

"Pirates! Pirates!" a messenger cried. Bouchard, the French pirate and his men attacked the Fort of Monterey in 1818. They burned buildings, killed people, and stole what they found. Would the pirates come to the Mission close by?

The padres and Indians were afraid. Quickly, they hid the treasures of the church and left. When the danger was over, they returned to find the Mission had not been touched.

When Father Fermin de Lasuen became President, he kept the plan of the mission system. He walked many miles to found nine other missions. He ruled the missions until the Mexican government took over.

TODAY AT THE MISSION

San Carlos Borromeo will long be remembered in history. Many a tired, hungry traveler would stop here for the night. There were no hotels in those days. This is where the presidents of the missions usually lived.

The old, worn leatherbound books in glass cases make up California's first library. Father Serra brought many of the books with him to the new country.

Reminders of him are everywhere. A statue shows him dying. His friends are gathered around him. The symbol of California, the grizzly bear, lies at his feet. A tiny, bare room like the one he lived in can be seen at the Mission.

Beautiful green gardens frame this Mission by the sea. Many visitors think this is the most beautiful of all the missions.

6

SAN ANTONIO DE PADUA

Third Mission, founded July 14, 1771

The Spaniards bent down to unpack their supplies. Two men lifted the bells and tied them to a tree. The Mission land had been chosen. Father Serra walked to the tree and pulled the ropes to ring the bells. They clanged loud and clear. "Come to God," he shouted into the forest. But no one was in sight except the Spaniards. Serra saw a young Indian boy coming towards them. He had heard the ringing of the bells. After the ceremony, Father Serra gave the boy gifts. He took them and went away. Later he came back with many other Indians.

Father Serra went on his way, leaving two padres in charge. A hard first year began with bad weather. Either the hot sun burned down on them or the freezing cold chilled them. Water dried up. The crops failed.

The next year, they moved the Mission near the San Miguel Creek. What a beautiful scene it made set among the mountains! Pine and oak trees grew on the land. The thumping noises of axes as they chopped down trees echoed in the valley. They used wood and dry brush to make shelters until adobe buildings could be built. Often the land chosen for the mission was not good enough. The soil would not grow crops. No stream or river flowed through the land for water. Many missions had to be moved for these reasons.

Each mission had to raise its own food and make goods in the workshops that it would need. The Spanish government would not give them money to run them.

Water flowed down the hills through clay pipes carrying it from the San Antonio River to the Mission. This long water pipe was called a water channel. It stretched for three miles. It brought water close to the fields for the crops.

One Easter in 1780, the wheat crop was almost destroyed by a cold frost. They kept flooding the fields with water to thaw it out. Then they prayed for nine days in the church. Their crop that year was a better one than ever before. This event helped give the Indians faith.

Beautiful Palomino horses galloped across the Mission lands shaking their manes in the wind. The Indians took pride in feeding, grooming, and caring for their prized horses. Everyone in California knew of Mission San Antonio's fine horses.

TODAY AT THE MISSION

The Mission looks like a small city today. Many of its buildings are rebuilt. The clanging of a blacksmith's tools at work is missing. Visitors can see where he made useful metal objects like saws and axes in his shop. In the tile workshops clay tiles for roofs and water pipes took their shape. Tools used by the Indians stand as models today. A saw with its sharp metal teeth cut through the rough logs. A grist mill was used for crushing wheat and making it into flour. An olive press squeezed olives for making olive oil.

The background of the Mission is set against a high mountain peak. Junipero Serra Peak is named for the founder of the missions. Sailors in the early days used it as a point to steer their ships toward. They gave the Mission gifts of carved wooden statues called figureheads from the ships to thank them for a safe journey.

rip saw

7

SAN GABRIEL ARCANGEL

Fourth Mission, founded September 8, 1771

The Spaniards came into view. Suddenly, a shower of arrows flew at them. The Indians were attacking! Quickly a padre pulled out the painting of Mary, Mother of Jesus. He held it up for the Indians to see.

What happened next seemed like a miracle. When the Indians saw the painting, they threw down their bows and arrows. They looked closely at its beauty. They offered the strangers their friendship. Now the painting is over three hundred years old. It is hung inside the church to remember that day.

The *Queen of the Missions* during its good times became the richest of all the missions. Great cattle herds wandered on the rich lands. Indians kept busy in the workshops. The soap workshop supplied many of the other missions with soap. More wine was made here than most missions.

But there was trouble at this Mission. One of their biggest problems was the soldiers. They were there to keep order, but they could not get along with the Indians. They made fun of them and tried to push them around. They punished them for little reasons. The Indians did not like this.

Once a soldier hurt the wife of an Indian chief. This made the chief angry. He gathered together a few members of his tribe and tried to attack the soldier. The soldiers fired their guns at the Indians, and the chief was killed.

The Indians were angry and so was Father Serra. This never should have happened. He told the governor in Mexico. The soldier was punished. But by then, the Indians did not trust the white man. For a long time, few Indians came to the Mission.

Settlers came from Mexico. They farmed and built towns called *pueblos* in California. Spain at this time owned Mexico and wanted more people to come to California. They wanted a strong claim to the land.

Settlers lived near the Mission in the nearby Pueblo of Los Angeles. Most of them were good people. Others caused problems. They hired Indians so they would not have to do the hard work of farming their land. The Indians were not paid much for their hard work.

The more troublesome of the settlers always complained. They said the padres did not take care of their religious needs. They said they cut off their water supply. Neither of the charges was true.

Governor Pio Pico claimed the land for Mexico. On May 4, 1846, he broke the law. He sold the Mission to pay his debts. San Gabriel was the Mission where he had been born and baptized!

TODAY AT THE MISSION

Visitors stop to feed the pigeons that flock in the courtyard and gardens. The church stands in the background.

Heavy supports hold it up against the many earthquakes that have shaken its walls. Four quakes shook the land on the day it was founded.

A famous collection of paintings hang on the walls. An unknown Christian Indian mixed paints and brushed them on the sails taken from a ship. Fourteen paintings tell the story of Jesus Christ. They are the oldest religious paintings by a California Indian.

A cannon called a *frijolera* (meaning a beanshooter) is one of the weapons that was used by the soldiers.

At one time the Mission lands grew to 90 acres. Times have changed. The nearby Pueblo of Los Angeles grew into the large City of Los Angeles. Cities of San Gabriel, Alhambra, and Monterey Park stand on soil that once belonged to the Mission.

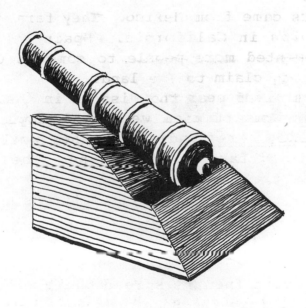

frijolera

8

SAN LUIS OBISPO DE TOLOSA

Fifth Mission, founded September 1, 1772

The generous Indians spread their wild nuts and grain on grass mats before the Spaniards to eat.

The hungry white men reached for handfuls of food. They chewed it noisily enjoying the taste. Finally, the hollow feeling in their stomachs filled up.

The Indians remembered when the white man had first come to this valley. Fierce bears roamed the land and scared them. Their simple bows and arrows could not hurt the bears' thick skins. The soldiers had come to hunt bear.

They had killed many. They had taken the meat back to the
hungry people of the Carmel and San Antonio Missions. The
Indians were thankful and friendly to the Spaniards.

Explorers carefully chose land watered by two streams
that flowed among the trees. The rich, brown soil would be
good for growing crops. Many friendly Indians lived here.
Maybe they would want to come to the Mission.

At first the Indians did not come. The Mission did not
have much to interest them. They were friendly but did not
care about the new religion. After the crops of corn and
beans were planted at the Mission, the Indians began to
come. Food sometimes interested the Indians and brought
them to the missions. They had to find their own. Sometimes there was much game and food to be found in the wilds.
Other times there was not.

There were also Indians that were not as friendly.
Three times the Mission was attacked by angry Indians. In
1776, 1778, and 1782 Indians shot fire arrows onto tule
grass roofs. Many of the buildings, food, and tools burned
up in these fires. Mission Indians helped to put the fires
out.

The reason these Indians attacked the Mission was they
believed the white man was their enemy. He was trying to
take their land. This was their way of showing the Spaniards they wanted them to go away.

But the Spaniards did not go away. They built more
buildings. They made tiles for roofs instead of grass.
These did not burn.

A warm, happy man named Father Luis Martinez came to
serve the Mission. The Indians gathered around him laughing
and talking. Sometimes he joined them in their games. His
friendliness brought many Indians to the Mission. He was a
brave man too. Once he led a group of Mission Indians to
defend several missions against possible attack by pirates.

"News from the padre," shouted the Indian man as he
ran into the courtyard. The men of the Indian village
gathered around to hear what he had to say.

"All workers meet tomorrow in the wheat field. Har-
vesting the crops will begin."

51

The man who spoke was an *alcalde*. By 1780 the Indians could elect these leaders called alcaldes. It was like we elect people today to represent us in government. During the day, alcaldes would visit the padres and learn the news and orders. At the end of the day, they would shout it out at the Indian villages. They also served as policemen to keep order among their people. *Regiodores* were less important leaders who helped them.

This was a good way for the Indians to learn how to govern themselves. The padres at the beginning hoped the Indians would be able to run the missions alone in time.

At first, the padres taught the Indians trades. During the 1790's, Mexican artists and workers came to teach crafts and trades to the Indians. They taught them ironwork, leathermaking, tanning, weaving, carpentry, and building.

The skills they taught were important in helping the missions support themselves.

The padre sat at his desk and dipped the point of his feather pen in the dark, black ink. Carefully he wrote on the paper. Wheat, 1300 bushels; corn, 300 bushels; and cattle, 700 head. On he wrote until he had put down all the crops and livestock of the Mission for that year.

He turned to the church records. How many people were born that year? How many were baptized, had married or died? The padre wrote it down. Then he closed the books. He was done for the year. Each year the government made a law that padres had to write these reports. It helps us know today how well the Mission did.

Indians at other missions became unhappy with their lives. The Chumash Indians at Santa Ines and La Purisima Missions attacked their missions. The Indians at San Luis Obispo seemed happy. They did not want to join in the attack.

Their happiness soon ended. The Mexican government took the Mission and arrested Father Martinez. They said things about him that were not true. They said he had taken money and killed Mission cattle. They said he was not loyal to Mexico. He was sent back to Spain by the Mexican government. They wanted to get rid of him. He could no longer protect the Indians. Some of the settlers took their land.

TODAY AT THE MISSION

Inside there are many art treasures to see. Carved wooden candleholders stand tall in the church. A metal and wooden bell wheel was turned with a handle. Photographs of the Mission show how it changed over the years. Indian baskets, arrowheads, and farm tools are shown. These are what the Indians used to do their work.

     Outside olive trees sway in the wind. They are the
first ones planted in California. Can you imagine the
Indians picking them back in mission days? Elementary and
high schools stand on the Mission land in the City of San
Luis Obispo.

9

SAN FRANCISCO DE ASIS (DOLORES)

Sixth Mission, founded June 26, 1776

A large expedition (group of people taking a long trip)
moved slowly toward San Francisco. Men, women, and children
came along with the padres and soldiers on the trip. The

hoof beats of the cattle could be heard as they plodded along the trail. The herd would be for the new Mission.

The people put up their tents near a lake and waited. Soon sailing ships would come with more people and supplies. They would build a *presidio* (fort) nearby.

No Indians came to the ceremony to bless the land for the Mission. Where had they gone? Enemy Indians had attacked and burned their village. Many of their people were killed. Others ran for the safety of a nearby land. A month later the Indians returned.

Many times later they came to visit the strangers. They took things from the new settlers. The soldiers fired their guns and hurt several Indians. For a while they feared the white people.

Mission Dolores never became a rich Mission. Many troubles disturbed the Mission. The weather was cold and foggy. The earth was sandy and not good for farming. They raised cattle to eat for food. The hides and tallow (animal fat) gave them products to trade to ships and other missions. The Indians made soap and candles from tallow.

Women were good at tanning animal hides. It took several weeks. They soaked them in lime water to loosen the hair. Then they scraped it off with a metal tool. The hide was stretched on the ground by pounding wooden stakes along the sides. It was left out in the sun to dry.

The Spaniards brought sickness to the Mission. The Indians' bodies shuddered from the fever and chills of measles and smallpox. They lived closely together so sickness spread quickly. This scared the Indians to see so many of their people dying. Many of them ran away. Only a few hundred Indians were left in ten years.

Something needed to be done! North of San Francisco the padres found land with good weather warmed by sunshine. It was quiet and peaceful in San Rafael. Buildings were built for another Mission. This one was more like a hospital. Sick Indians came here to rest. Many Indians got well.

Should Mission Dolores be closed? This question was asked. With all its problems and bad weather, it might be best. The government and padres argued. Finally, they decided to keep it open.

The Costonoans Indians who lived here fished for much of their food. Waves crashed against their canoes. Quickly they steered their boats through the foamy water. They dipped their baskets and nets into the sea to catch sardines. They made fishhooks from shells. With these they caught whitefish, sea-bream, and other kinds of fish. The Indians also carved spears of bone to catch fish.

Costonoan Indians paddled their canoes out to fish

TODAY AT THE MISSION

Mission Dolores was a lonely spot in mission days. Few travelers came here. The Gold Rush finally woke up this sleepy village. It turned it into the busy City of San Francisco.

The old Mission church now stands next to a new one. Inside the old one the Indian artwork is still bright. The ceiling is painted in colors of red, blue, white, and yellow. The new church is large and beautifully decorated. Many people worship here today. The two churches stand side by side. One tells of the past life. The other tells of the present.

10
SAN JUAN CAPISTRANO

Seventh Mission, founded November 1, 1776

Eight days after the Mission founding, a horseman galloped into their camp. "Indian attack, Indian attack!" he shouted. "Mission San Diego is on fire!"

The padres at San Juan Capistrano did not know if they would be attacked too. They quickly buried the mission bells and hurried to the fort at San Diego. The soldiers there would protect them. The Mission would have to wait to be founded.

A year later the padres came back. Many Indians came to the Mission within a short time. This Mission enjoyed success from the beginning. Acres of fruit trees were planted in long rows. Juicy red and green grapes grew on the vines. The good crops fed the people well.

The Mission community was a busy place to live. The Indians worked at their trades in the indoor and outdoor workshops. They spun, wove, sewed, and carved wood. They became good wagon-makers, blacksmiths, shoemakers, winemakers, and olive-oil makers.

Many herds of cattle roamed the grassy lands. Hides from cattle were stretched in the sun to dry. They were made into leather goods such as saddles and sandals. Sometimes they were traded to other missions.

Every part of the cattle was used. The fat and bones were boiled down into tallow in brick pits. They made soap and candles from it.

In the blacksmith's shop they made metal objects like locks, keys, and iron bars. The smelter was a brick pit used to heat the metal.

An olive crusher made olive oil. First the Indians washed the olives and stuffed them into woolen bags. They put them in a press and turned it. Out came the olive oil. It was used for cooking in the Mission kitchen, lamps, and trade.

The story of this Mission is one of growth. Indians kept coming and buildings kept being built. Soon the many people could no longer fit into the tiny chapel.

The biggest and most beautiful church of the missions would be built. A fine stone builder drew up the plans. The church was to be built in the shape of a cross.

Everyone wanted to help build it. Men, women, and children all carried stones from several miles away. The yellow stone was called sandstone. The church took many years to build. A great celebration followed. It lasted for two whole days. Many people came, even the governor.

Only a few years later, in 1812, an earthquake struck. The dome ceiling came tumbling down. It crashed on top of the people during a church service. Sadly, all forty Indians were killed.

TODAY AT THE MISSION

The swallows build their mud nests in the ruins of the church. Their flights are famous. Crowds of people gather to watch them. The birds always fly South for the cold winter on October 23rd. Cheering people welcome them back to the Mission every March 19th. They are never late.

Father Serra's chapel is still standing. It is the oldest church in California. Many art objects from early days are inside. An altar is made of red cherry wood and carved by hand. Around it are other religious objects such as wooden statues and crosses. There is an old stone baptismal bowl with a wooden cover. The mud-colored adobe brick walls are four-feet thick. Over the years the bright colors of the Indians' art has become lighter. The walls have been brushed with more paint to make them look like before.

Visitors, artists, and photographers visit the Mission. Flowers are in bloom. Young and old people like the green gardens, long adobe hallways, and sparkling fountains. It is one of the most beautiful.

11

SANTA CLARA DE ASIS

Eighth Mission, founded January 12, 1777

Tall on a hill stood a church for religious women to live in called a convent. It was faraway in the mountains. Saint Claire lived there after founding an order (group) of nuns. She wanted to live her life in service to God. Her parents did not want her to. At eighteen she ran away to do this. Mission Santa Clara is named after her. Each mission is named after a saint. This is the first mission to be named after a woman.

The soldiers and a few Indians began to build the Mission. They molded adobe bricks of clay earth. The walls went up slowly with few Indians to help. Not many cared for the Mission.

When the Spaniards had first come, the Indians were hungry and took some of their mules for food. Soldiers followed them to their village and fought with them. They took some of the Indian leaders back and beat them. Then the Indians did not want to come to the Mission.

Sickness spread through the land. Many of the Indian children died. Their parents brought their children to be baptized hoping to save them from death.

Santa Clara was a mission that had to struggle. Rain poured down most of the first winter. Water in the Guadalupe River rose higher and higher. It came over the top and rushed out, flooding over the buildings. This was not the last time it was to happen. A second time floods washed away buildings. An earthquake hit and crumbled them away again.

A few months after the Mission was founded, settlers came. They built the Pueblo (town) of San Jose across the river from the Mission. Problems grew between the settlers and the people at the Mission. Cattle wandered back and forth between the two places. Who owned them? Where did Mission land end and Pueblo land begin? They argued about it. There were many arguments that needed to be settled.

A row of trees stood on either side of the road. It was called *The Alameda*. It was four miles long and joined the town and the Mission. On Sundays men drove their wives and families to the Mission church in carriages pulled by horses.

One of the reasons the Indians came to the Mission was Father Jose Viader. He was a tall, big man with a kind heart. One night three Indians crept into his room. They tried to beat him. The padre was so strong he fought them all off and won. He gave them a strict talk on how badly they had acted. Then he forgave them and became their friend.

Another padre named Father Magin Catala lived at the Mission. The Indians called him *El Profesta*, which means "The Prophet" in English. They believed he could tell them the future. Some say he told them Spain would no longer rule the land. He said gold would be found in California. Both things did happen.

TODAY AT THE MISSION

In the good times the Mission lands grew wonderful fruit. Orange and palm trees sway in the wind today. Red rosebushes bloom in the garden. Though the buildings are gone, the trees still are here.

Heavy rains washed the adobe buildings away. A blazing fire burned down other buildings.

The University of Santa Clara now stands on the land. This school began in early California. A museum has objects from those times. An old metal bell was once a present to the Mission from the King of Spain. It was carried all the way from Spain to California by ship. In the glass case is a padre's diary (notebook). The Mission Register that told of the records of the Mission in animals, Indians, and goods is there. A new church was built to look like the old one.

12

SAN BUENAVENTURA

Ninth Mission, founded March 31, 1782

On Easter Sunday, Father Serra raised the wooden cross and blessed it. Under a brushwood shelter the first church service took place.

At last San Buenaventura had been founded! For many years it was put off. The San Gabriel Mission Indians fought against the soldiers because they were treated unfairly by them. The governor sent more soldiers to protect the Mission. Then there were not enough soldiers to protect the padres to found a new mission.

When the Spaniards came, they found the Chumash Indians to be very clever and friendly. They lived in houses made of tule grass and slept on beds filled with straw. The men were skilled at making large canoes from wood. The women were known for the beauty of their basketmaking.

The Spaniards watched as the Indians made their houses in a cone shape. The Indians picked strong tree branches and cut them down for poles. They stuck the poles deep in the ground in the shape of a circle. Then they dug out the earth inside it. Bending the tops of the poles, they tied them together with leather strips. Women wove mats of grass for the outside of the hut. The mats were joined to the poles to form the walls. The top was left open so smoke from the fire could come out.

The Indians quickly accepted Christianity and helped the Spaniards build the Mission. Their buildings could not stand up to the strong shaking of earthquakes. The Earthquake of 1812 hit, and the bell tower fell down. A huge wave called a tidal wave swept close to the Mission. It nearly washed it away. All over California buildings crumbled. Many people were killed.

The earth at the Mission was dry. It needed water for crops to grow. The Indians made clay pipes to bring water to the land. This made them able to grow some unusual crops. Bananas, sugar cane, figs, and coconuts could be found on the lands.

Mission Indians were not supposed to trade with Indians who were not Christians. The padres feared they would go back to their villages and their old ways.

In 1818, Mojave Indians who were not Christians came to the Mission. They came to trade. The padres found out about it. They ordered the Indians thrown in jail. The angry Indians fought with the soldiers. Several Indians were killed. This event caused bad feelings among the Indians.

After the United States took over California, the Mission became a Catholic church. One priest decided to paint it. He covered up the beautiful Indian paintings on the walls. He took away art and objects from early days. It is too bad only the adobe walls and a side door are all that is left of the Indians' work.

TODAY AT THE MISSION

Many unusual objects can be seen in the Mission museum. An elephant hip bone is left over from the days of the dinosaurs. Scientists digging in the Mission ruins were surprised to find it.

The old wooden bell lined with metal comes from the bell tower. This is the only mission that did not use iron bells.

Tools from the blacksmith's shop, a church lamp, Indians' baskets, and farming tools are some of the less unusual objects.

Clothes of fine materials are colorfully woven with flowers in gold and red threads. They belonged to the padres and were worn for church services.

When the railroad came, the town of Ventura grew. The church and garden are all that is left of the Mission.

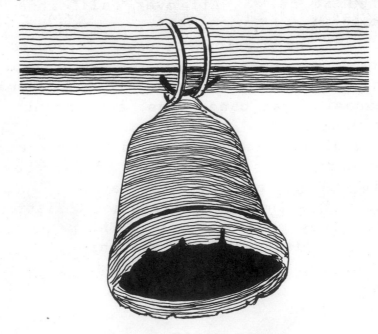

13

SANTA BARBARA

Tenth Mission, founded December 4, 1786

Father Serra was happy and excited! A fort at Santa Barbara soon would be built. Though permission had not come, a mission was planned to be built near it. Father Serra joined the soldiers on their journey. He chose the land for the Mission and blessed it. But the government did not give permission. Several more years of waiting would pass before this would happen. Father Serra did not know that Governor Felipe de Neve was against the way the mission system was run.

He wanted another plan. He thought they should send one padre instead of two. The padre would live alone in a house built next to the chapel. A few soldiers would guard him. No mission was to be built where the Indians would come to live. The padre would visit them in their villages. Here he would teach them about Christianity.

This system was tried in Colorado the year before. It failed and many padres were killed by Indians. Father Serra fought against the governor's plan. He would not let this same thing happen in California. Years later permission for the founding of the new Mission came.

Only one out of three Indians became Christians in early California. The Chumash of this area welcomed the Spaniards. They helped them build adobe buildings. Many clung to their old ways and built grass huts to live in at the Indian village. Later they lived in adobes too.

Orange and olive trees grew in long rows called orchards. A water system brought water to the rich fields of wheat, barley, corn, beans, and peas. It brought it to the Mission where it poured out of a stone fountain shaped like a bear's head. The water filled up into a basin (tub) where the women washed clothes. They spent many hours talking with each other as they scrubbed their families' clothes clean.

On February 21, 1824 an Indian rider came with news from Santa Ines Mission. A soldier had beaten an Indian without good reason. The Indians were fighting against the soldiers. Would the Santa Barbara Indians like to join the fight?

The Mission Indians talked among themselves. The soldiers often punished them too harshly. They laughed at them. They brought sicknesses many Indians died from. Life at the Mission seemed stricter everyday. There were so many rules to follow. The padres made them work so hard. Yes, they decided, they would join the attack.

Quickly, the Indian men sent the women and children off into the hills for safety. Then they attacked the Mission. Bullets flew through the air. Indians and soldiers fought with each other. Finally, the fighting calmed down and the Indians escaped. They ran up in the hills to join their families. They took up with the warlike Tulare Indians. Only a few old Indians stayed behind.

What was a mission without Indians? Nothing. The padres had no one to teach Christianity to. The work came to a stop. The padre went to the Indians and begged them to come back. After four months, many went back. Others did not ever want to.

TODAY AT THE MISSION

The Mission sits high on a hill looking over the beach town of Santa Barbara. The design of the building is beautiful and unusual. It looks like old Greek and Roman buildings.

Before the padre built it, he turned through pages of many books. What did he know about building? Not very much. He decided to learn. He helped the Indians build the fine church out of yellow stone. It took five years to build. Two tall towers stand on each side of it.

This is the only mission that has always had a padre living here to look after it. This is why the buildings are in good shape.

It is fun to walk around the garden. Can you find the fountain and basin where Indian women washed the clothes?

The buildings have been used for a high school, junior college, and a school for priests. Bells ring only on Sundays. They ring to call people to worship in the church.

14

LA PURISIMA CONCEPCION

Eleventh Mission, founded December 8, 1787

Success of a mission depended on many things. Good land and plenty of water was necessary for growing crops. There should be friendly Indians and kind, wise padres. Skilled trades needed to be learned and developed. Many herds of animals must be raised to help feed the people. La Purisima had all of these.

The land was carefully chosen. It was in a valley near a river. Father Lasuen planted the cross. The founding of this Mission had been put off. Governor Neve did not want the padres to teach the Indians anything but religion.

Golden pears hung from the many fruit trees at the Mission. Green and red grapes spilled over grapevines. This Mission was famous for its fruits. From the grapes, they made wine.

They made important products in the workshops. Candles and soap were made from tallow (animal fat). Rough cloth and blankets were woven from wool. They skillfully cut and shaped leather into saddles and harnesses for horses. They made shoes for the people.

The beginning of their troubles started with the Earthquake of 1812. All over California the ground shook. The walls of the Mission swayed. Cracks opened in the walls. The people were afraid. What was happening? After the first quake, the padres looked the buildings over. Just then another quake hit. The buildings shook even harder. This time they fell down. Heavy rains followed and washed the broken ruins away.

Their problems never stopped. The land dried out when the rain did not come. Crops failed. A very cold winter killed hundreds of sheep. A fire burned down many Indian huts. Measles, smallpox, and other sicknesses killed many Indians. Their friend Father Mariano Payeras died. The Indians felt sad and discouraged.

At this time the war between Mexico and Spain was going on. It brought hardship to their lives. No supplies came to the Mission. The Indians had to make more goods since none were coming in. They worked even harder than before. They had little freedom. The soldiers treated them worse. The government would not pay the soldiers anymore for their jobs. This was because of the war. The soldiers often took their problems out on the Indians.

What else could go wrong? News came from the Santa Ines Mission of the Indian attack on that mission. These Indians at La Purisima were ready. They had put away food, supplies, and guns. They attacked their own Mission and took charge of it for a month.

More soldiers came to fight against them. Another battle began. They fought for two and a half hours. There were too many soldiers. Finally, the Indians had to give up. Indians who did not want to fight against the Mission had hidden in the mountains. They came back after the fighting was over mainly because they had nowhere else to go.

Later, the Mission lands were sold. Through the years, they changed hands many times. The Mission became a stable for animals. In the Old West times it was a saloon and a hideout for outlaws.

TODAY AT THE MISSION

Mission ranches and farms are gone. Only a few walls were standing when the State of California took it over. Now they own it and keep it running.

Animals are fenced in pens outside. They remind the visitors of the many animals that once roamed the lands.

Outdoor and indoor workshops have been rebuilt. A weaving room has a wooden loom. The clay pipes from the water channel wind down from the hills. This Mission is one of the most fully rebuilt ones. It is an interesting one to visit near the City of Lompoc.

15

SANTA CRUZ

Twelfth Mission, founded August 28, 1791

The sun shone down and sparkled on the clear, blue water. Indian children ran into the waves. They splashed each other. On the shore other children played their favorite game of hoop and pole. A player threw the pole through the round hoop. It landed in the hoop. This gave the player points. The children cheered. Others spun tops made from acorns near the Mission.

The view from the Mission was beautiful! It overlooked the water. The land chosen seemed perfect. Good weather and rich soil and plenty of water. Trees in the forest and stone nearby could be used for building the Mission.

The early years passed happily by. Grains, fruits, and vegetables grew on the lands. Many Indians came to live at the Mission. But trouble came to change this success.

Settlers came to live across the river at the town of Branciforte. Some of the people who came were not honest. They caused trouble at the Mission.

Fear of pirates spread to Santa Cruz. Monterey nearby had been attacked and set on fire in 1818. Would the pirates come here?

The governor ordered the priest and Indians to leave the Mission. They followed orders and went to Mission Soledad. There they would be safe.

The settlers across the river were told to hide the Mission valuables. The pirates never came, but some of the settlers did. The priest and Indians returned and found all the Mission's valuable goods were gone. The priest was angry! He reported the theft at once to the governor. But the people never returned them. The priest said he would leave the Mission. But the church would not let him.

One night an Indian asked another padre to visit a sick Indian. The padre was in the orchard. He did not want to go back to the Mission to wake up a soldier to go with him. He went with the Indian. On his way home, he was attacked and killed by several other Indians. The Indians were punished, but they said the padre had treated them badly.

Through these troubled times farming and herds of animals did well. Many Indians became discouraged with Mission life and left. The Mission could not go on without them. Mexico came to power and sent an administrator (a person to run it) to take over the lands. He divided it up among the settlers.

TODAY AT THE MISSION

What began as a "perfect" Mission ended as a total failure. The soldiers' living quarters is the only building still standing. The church is new, built to look like the old Mission. *Santa Cruz* means "sacred cross" in Spanish. Its name stands for the symbol of Christianity. Mission lands and the town of Branciforte are now part of the beach community of Santa Cruz.

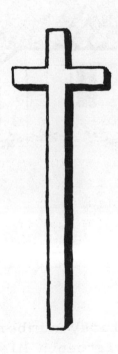

16

NUESTRA SENORA DE LA SOLEDAD

Thirteenth Mission, founded October 9, 1791

Thirteen is an unlucky number. Some people believe this. Soledad is the thirteenth Mission to be founded. Was it unlucky? Why did it fail?

The story of the Mission began many years before it was founded. Captain Portola and Father Juan Crespi came and camped here for the night. They were looking for land on which to build another mission.

An Indian came by. He spoke to them. He said the same word over and over again. It sounded like *soledad*. The visitors knew the word meant "loneliness" in Spanish. They looked around them. There were no trees. The land was flat. No one else was in sight. They agreed with the Indian. It was a lonely place.

Twenty-two years later another padre came. Father Lasuen founded the Mission. Very few Indians lived around here. This was unusual. Missions were usually built near a large number of Indian villages.

This Mission was needed to be built for another reason too. Many people walked in the days of early California. Others traveled by horse. They all needed a resting place. This Mission would be a day's walk between the San Jose and San Carlos Missions.

It took a while to build up the number of Indians at the Mission. Costonoan Indians near the ocean were too faraway. Building went slowly. The few people worked as hard as they could.

The Mission had many troubles. Farming did not do well. The people brought water from the Salinas River through clay pipes. Still the crops did not grow. Sometimes too little rain fell. At other times it poured down. When this happened, the river flooded its banks. It ruined crops and destroyed buildings three different times.

The herds of sheep and horses and cattle grew. This helped to feed the Mission Indians.

The bad weather and troubles made this a mission where most padres did not want to come. The rooms were cold in the winter. They baked in the summer heat. A sickness called *The Plague* killed many Indians. Many left to find a better life.

All these problems placed a heavy load on the padres. Padres came and went. They asked to go to other missions. No padre stayed longer than four years. They were not happy here.

Other padres wanted to help. Padre Ibanez came to the Mission. The Indians liked him because he was gentle and good to them. He taught them to read and write. He took care of them when they were sick. He loved and respected them.

Another padre came later whose name was Father Francisco de Sarria. He hoped to change the troubles of the Mission. He loved the Indians and tried to keep the Mission going. The crops failed and there was little food. He often gave his share to the Indians. Sadly, he died of hunger. The Indians buried him and left the Mission. With the kind padre gone, they did not want to stay.

TODAY AT THE MISSION

Buildings fell down, and the roof was sold. All that was left of the Mission was the front part of the chapel. Now this little white chapel has been rebuilt and also the padres' rooms. A fiesta is given every year to try to raise money to help rebuild more of the Mission.

17

SAN JOSE DE GUADALUPE

Fourteenth Mission, founded June 11, 1797

Another rest stop was needed. The Indians on this land were against the soldiers and travelers riding through. Maybe if a mission could be built, they would be friendlier. The land was chosen two years before they built the Mission.

What should it be called? Everyone thought up a different name. Father Antonio Daniti who chose it called it *San Francisco Solano* for a stream he named nearby. The

Indians called it *Oroysom*. The governor of the territory (land) called it *The Alameda*.

The governor in Mexico decided he would get to choose the name since he was the highest government leader. He said it would be called *San Carlos Borromeo*. Quickly, someone told him there already was a California mission with that name! To cover his embarrassment, he gave it a new name, *San Jose*.

The founding ceremony must have been quite a sight to see. They tried to interest the Indians so they would come to the Mission. Everyone dressed in their best clothes. Soldiers, padres, and Indians from other missions came. Father Lasuen began the ceremony. He sprinkled holy water on the land and blessed it. A wooden cross was planted in the ground. The soldiers raised the flag of Spain. They fired their guns. The worship service then took place. Many Indians watched.

The nearby Santa Clara Mission gave them many animals. They drove cattle and horses, mules and oxen, sheep and bulls along the trail. Mission Dolores sent them animals too. Older missions usually gave what they could to new missions just starting out. Soldiers began to build the first buildings. The Mission was off to a good start.

Not many Indians came. They liked their lives and the freedom to roam.

But one adult Indian woman wanted to be baptized. Fathers Barcenilla and Merino were new padres. How did they baptize someone? They did not know. Quickly, they sent a messenger to Mission Santa Clara. Father Magin de Catala came to help. He showed them how and wrote down the woman's new name of Josefa in the baptism book.

As time went on, the Indians changed their minds. They came from miles away to live at the Mission. Their numbers grew to 6,737 Indians. They had more Indians than any other mission but Mission San Luis Rey.

Many outbreaks of fighting took place. An Indian ran to the priest, telling him of sick, runaway Indians that needed his help. He begged the priest to come. A group of soldiers and a few Mission Indians went with the padre into the mountains. On the way they were attacked by Indians. Only four people came back alive. Among them was the wounded padre.

Jedediah Smith was a famous American explorer and fur trader. He came with a group of men and trapped furs. After an Indian attack, they came to the Mission for help.

Another time a Mission Indian named Estanislao ran away. He did not like the Mission. He wandered among the runaway Indians talking and planning against the Mission. One night they attacked the Mission. Soldiers jumped out of their beds and grabbed their guns. They fired at the Indians. The Indians shot back but lost in the end. The padre forgave them. Estanislao and many others came back to live at the Mission.

It was sold in 1846 but later left alone by its owners. Americans and travelers alike used it during the Gold Rush. It became a stable. Then someone turned it into a saloon. Another time it was used for a store. People stole the Mission treasures. Buildings crumbled and fell down. An earthquake totally destroyed it.

TODAY AT THE MISSION

Now it is a small reminder of the once busy community. The museum is made from the only building left. This was once an important mission with many crops and animals.

Music filled the Mission then. The Indians liked to play the musical instruments. Father Narciso Duran showed them how to play the ones the Spaniards brought. The Indians practiced in a group of thirty people called an orchestra. They got so good that they became famous. People used to come from miles away to hear them play. The Mission is 15 miles away from the City of San Jose.

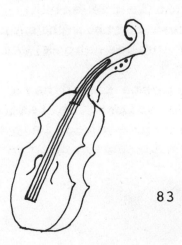

18

SAN JUAN BAUTISTA

Fifteenth Mission, founded June 24, 1797

Little did the padres know where they had built their
Mission. On top of the biggest earthquake fault in Califor-
nia! A fault is a weak spot in the earth. The land cracks
and the earth moves back and forth. This one is called the
San Andreas Fault. Many quakes shook this land and the
Mission.

Father Arroyo de la Cuesta tried hard to interest the
Indians in coming to the Mission. He learned over twelve
languages. In church he preached in seven different
languages. He wanted them to understand the new religion.

The Indians who came to the Mission were given new Christian names. He liked to give them names of famous people from history. He named them after kings like Alexander and great leaders like Plato.

Indians kept on coming. Men, women, and children squeezed into the church. So many came that a bigger church needed to be built. The padres made plans. It took a long time to build. By then times had changed. Many Indians had died or left the Mission. There no longer were enough Indians to fill it. They had to put up a wall to make it smaller.

Everyone enjoyed music at the Mission. One of the padres knew all about music. Father Estevan Tapis even wrote his own music. Singing voices filled the church. The padre used a special way to teach the Indians music. He colored the notes in red, white, black, and yellow. Each person learned their part by following their own color. Music became an important part of their lives. Once it saved them.

Unfriendly Indians attacked the Mission. The padre ran to the barrel organ and began to play. Beautiful sounds came from the organ pipes. The padre's idea worked. The attacking Indians were surprised. What was this strange object? They laid down their bows and arrows and began to explore it. Never had they seen anything like it. They listened to the sounds that came like magic from the wooden box. They forgot about fighting and wanted to stay.

85

This rich Mission had many herds of animals, good farming, and many Indians. Time brought this to an end.

TODAY AT THE MISSION

The earthquake damage to the building can be seen on the side of the walls. Steel and concrete beams make the building stronger in case of other earthquakes. An old metal bell that hung from the bell tower is left.

Inside the church the altar was carved by hand. A sailor named Thomas Doak painted it in blue and red. He had left his ship. Another worker said he would paint it for 75 cents a day. Doak needed a place to stay and food to eat so he painted it for free. He liked California so well, he decided to stay. This made him the first American to settle here.

Stone tools and woven baskets are shown from the early days. For many years the Indian women used these stone to grind corn and grain for their families.

This life is gone. Today we can see the Mission. Next to it are a stable, two adobe houses, and a hotel. All look like they did in the times of early California.

19
SAN MIGUEL ARCANGEL

Sixteenth Mission, founded July 25, 1797

The Indians eagerly waited for the day when the padres would come. This was unusual. Many of their friends and relatives lived happily on other missions. They heard good things about the missions. The expedition came. By the end of the first day, the padres had baptized fifteen Indian children.

Buildings went up fast with the willing Indians helping. People knew more about building now, and it was not as hard to do. Other missions sent the animals and supplies needed to begin the Mission. Several Indian families came from other missions to help.

A smooth beginning ended with trouble from their padre, Father Horra. He did not like missionary life. He grew lonely so far away from the other padres and a town. The heat and numerous ants bothered him. Each day got worse. He hated it more and could not fit in. Then he started doing strange things. He fired guns and scared off some of the Indians. The padre went insane and was sent home to Spain.

A fire broke out in 1806. The storehouses burned to the ground. The Mission's supply of wheat was destroyed. Workshops burned down so Indians could not make what they needed. Nearby missions helped. They sent all the supplies they could spare to help the Mission.

Life soon returned to normal. They could start to build. The roofs they made now were tile. They would not burn. This Mission got so good at making tiles that they were known for trading them with other missions. Soon after they started to rebuild, the war between Mexico and Spain brought more hard times.

Father Ramon Abella came in 1841. There was not enough food to feed the Mission. A year later they found him lying on a bed weak from hunger. He was still sharing what little food he had with the Indians.

San Miguel was the last Mission to be sold in 1846. It was bought only a few days before the United States took over. The new owner was named William Reed. He moved his family into the Mission and opened a store. Travelers passing through stopped for several days to rest. Reed was not wise. He liked to talk about his money. He told them about the gold he had made in the mines and money he had from selling cattle and sheep. The greedy visitors robbed him and killed everyone at the Mission.

TODAY AT THE MISSION

Bright colors are painted on the walls inside the church today. There are two old chairs. One is called the *wishing chair*. There is a story told about it. Once a padre asked a young Indian girl to sit in the chair.

"Wish for anything you want," he told her.

The girl sat down and thought. "I wish for a wonderful husband," she said.

The padre told her that her wish would come true. The same year it did. After this, many Indians believed in the magic of the chair.

The museum shows a model of the San Miguel Mission and what it looked like long ago. Indian arrowheads, jewelry, and baskets can be seen. The iron soldiers' swords shine in glass cases. The Mission is near the town of San Miguel.

20

SAN FERNANDO REY DE ESPANA

Seventeenth Mission, founded September 8, 1797

San Fernando became one of the largest missions. Older missions gave them a good start. They gave them horses, mules, cattle, sheep, and oxen. The herds grew bigger.

Raising cattle became their most important work. The Indians kept coming too. Everything went well.

During the year 1797, the padres founded four missions. This was one of them. These missions filled up the gaps in the mission chain. The plan was that each mission would be built a day's walk from the next one.

The Indians skillfully developed the trades. The blacksmith pounded metal into tools, plows, branding irons,

and fancy ironwork. He made horseshoes for the mules and horses at the Mission.

The Indians were famous for their grapes. The padres brought the vines all the way from Spain to plant. They grew well in the good weather. Indians picked the plump, ripe, juicy grapes. They hauled them by oxcart from the fields to the Mission. Then they threw them in pits called vats. After washing their feet, they climbed on top of the grapes. They squished them with their feet. Juice poured out of the bottom of the vat from a wooden pipe. They gathered and stored the juice in oxhides in the cellar. There it turned into wine. Later they used wooden barrels to hold the wine. The wine was used for many things. They needed it for church services, drink, and for medicine. It could be traded with the outside world and other missions.

Hard times came upon this Mission as with the rest. Their lives became difficult during the war. If only the soldiers earned their own living. They could have planted crops and hunted for game, but they did not. They depended on the Indians to feed and make them what they needed.

Many government leaders lived here. The famous Governor Pio Pico who was against the missions and sold them when Mexico took over lived here. John Fremont, an American explorer of the West also stayed at this Mission.

Gold was found here six years before the Gold Rush. A mission administrator was looking for onions in the field for his dinner. When he pulled them up, he found gold dust. Many people came looking for gold. Not much was found.

TODAY AT THE MISSION

Paintings and photographs of the Mission have many stories to tell. A Mission Indian painted others as they worked in the fields gathering grapes.

A painting of Saint Francis of Asisi hangs in the Mission. This painting was almost lost. A man saw it first as a sign, "Hay for sale," the sign read. The man stopped to look at the sign. He turned it over. This painting was on the other side. He gave it back to the Mission.

There are books on many subjects in the library. Books on farming, building, geography, and religion stand on shelves. Others explain skilled crafts and trades. The daily lives of the people depended on the information found in these books.

Look for holes cut in the large Mission doors. These were for the cats to go in and out. When this Mission had trouble with rats eating their grain, they borrowed cats from the San Gabriel Mission. The cats did a good job of catching the rats.

Today, houses of the San Fernando Valley are built around the old Mission.

21
SAN LUIS REY DE FRANCIA

Eighteenth Mission, founded June 13, 1789

Birds sang from their trees in the gardens. Pear, apple, and peach trees grew tall. The first pepper tree planted in California shaded this Mission.

Out in the fields the Indians planted wheat, corn, and beans every year. They gathered a large crop of grain. Only the San Gabriel Mission grew more crops. Their herds reached 27,000 head of cattle and 26,000 sheep. They had more than any other mission.

As time passed, they added many buildings. Three thousand Indians came to the Mission. There were more Indians here too.

The padre built the church in the shape of a cross. The tall bell tower served as a lookout to warn them of strangers. Indians waved flags to workers in the fields. This was a sign which told them how many sheep and cattle should be brought to the mission the following day.

Inside the church was a small chapel in the corner. It was where the Indians came to pray for their dead.

Father Antonio Peyri lived at the Mission for many years. He was a kind man the Indians liked. When the Mexican government took over, they told the padre to leave. He would have to go back to Spain. He loved the Indians and did not want to have to say goodbye. He left late at night when everyone was asleep. Two young Indian boys went with him. When the others discovered him gone, they followed him. They begged him to return. He knew he could not. From the ship, he waved a sad goodbye.

Father Peyri still hoped he could help the Indians. The two bright Indian boys who came with him to Spain he sent to school. One of them called Pablo Tac wanted to become a priest. He wrote down the story of his life in a book. This was the only known record to be written by a mission Indian.

TODAY AT THE MISSION

Rooms at the Mission show the daily lives of the people who lived there.

The padres' rooms are plain and simple. A wooden bed is one of the few pieces of furniture. A wool blanket rests at the foot. Above it hangs a carved wooden cross made by Indians. Beside it hangs the padre's gray robe he wore everyday. The yellow straw hat is next to it. This is what he used to shade his eyes from the sun. A water pitcher made out of clay sits on the old wooden table. He used it to wash his face.

On the wall of the kitchen hang many metal pots used for cooking. The brick ovens are not used anymore. Once they were packed with wood and lit to make a fire. Meals for the Mission were cooked here. A large, flat stone and a smaller round one were used for grinding corn and grain.

Candles hang from the ceiling in the tallow room. Pieces of string were tied on a wheel. The candlemaker poured melted tallow on each string. Then he turned the wheel and did the next one. He let the tallow cool and poured on more. The candles kept on getting bigger. When the candles were done, they were used in church and to light the dark rooms.

San Luis Rey is called the *King of the Missions*. The name fits because this is the largest of all of the missions.

22

SANTA INES

Nineteenth Mission, founded September 17, 1804

A fiesta was about to begin. A party to honor Saint
Ines. This saint was the one for whom the Mission was

named. Everyone arose early. The church service was held.
This marked the beginning of each day at the Mission. Now
the people gathered around to watch the games. The Indians
played a game much like field hockey with a wooden ball.
They raced against each other to see who could run the
fastest. Bullfights brought crowds. At night everyone
listened to musicians play in the Mission orchestra. Laughing, singing, and music filled the air. Many people began
to dance. Nobody worked that day.

The next morning work began as usual. The skilled
Indians could be proud of their work. They were good farm-
ers. Their herds of cattle grew to 13,000 head. They did
well at many trades. Their leather and iron crafts were
famous.

Santa Ines became a school. Young pioneer men came
here to study. This was the first college in California.

The smooth running of the Mission was stopped by the
war with Spain in 1810. The soldiers did not get paid after
that. They were angry and took it out on the Indians. The
soldiers were called "leather jackets" because they wore
heavy quilted hide coats. These protected them from the
Indians' arrows. The soldiers also had rifles, swords, and
hide shields for protection. They had much stronger weapons
than the Indians.

When the Earthquake of 1812 rocked the Mission, the
church was nearly destroyed. Other buildings fell down.
Much time was spent rebuilding. A new and larger church was
made of adobe and brick. Wood from pine trees nearby was
used to make the walls stronger. A roof was made from
tiles.

Trouble came on February 21, 1824. With little reason,
a soldier harshly beat a young Indian man. The Indians
became angry. They did not like this. There were many
other times the soldiers were rough with them. The Indians
set fire to the Mission. They attacked the soldiers but
left the padres alone.

This attack stirred the countryside! A few Indians rode to the nearby missions of La Purisima and Santa Barbara. They told others at these missions what had happened. The Indians at La Purisima and Santa Barbara decided to fight the soldiers too.

After the fighting ended, many Indians hid in the mountains. They joined the Tulare Indian tribe and lived among them. Only a few Indians ever came back.

Much later the Mission buildings fell to ruin, though they were still used. A priest was preaching from his pulpit (stand) when he felt it crumbling under him. It crashed to the ground. Though not hurt, he was very surprised.

TODAY AT THE MISSION

The Danish-American town of Solvang has grown up around this Mission. Fine examples of mission arts and crafts can be seen here. Handmade leather seats, a copper bowl, objects in brass and gold and silver are among the art treasures. Beautiful paintings hang in the church.

Walk in the garden. The many colorful flowers bloom all year. The garden is built in the shape of a cross. A water fountain sparkles in the center.

23

SAN RAFAEL ARCANGEL

Twentieth Mission, founded December 14, 1817

San Rafael Arcangel was named for the angel of healing.
It was started as an asistencia or branch mission for

Mission Dolores. They needed a hospital branch where their their sick Indians could go to get well.

Father Ramon Abella of Mission Dolores wrote a letter to Governor Sola for help. Many of the Indians were dying. They had caught "white men's sicknesses" like measles and chicken pox and smallpox. The cold and rainy weather of San Francisco made other Indians sick.

The governor wrote back. What they needed was a place to live where it was warmer. San Rafael was where the Indians would go.

From the beginning, San Rafael was built to be simple not beautiful. One long building divided it into many rooms. A small, plain church was built.

Father Gil knew something about medicine. He was chosen to head the branch. Under his care the Indians became well.

Next, another priest named Father Juan Amoros, took over and taught the Indians trades. They learned to plant crops and care for animals. The Indians worked hard to help the Mission grow. This interested many Indians living nearby to come to live here. The padre asked for permission for San Rafael Arcangel to become a full mission. On October 19, 1822, it became one.

The Indians at Mission San Rafael liked their lives and were happy. Father Jose Mercado came and changed that. He was strict with the Indians and lost his temper often. He argued and made trouble among the soldiers.

Once he thought warlike Indians were planning to attack the Mission. Giving the Mission Indians guns, he sent them out to find the unfriendly Indians before they could attack. Many good Indians were needlessly killed in the battle. The church punished the padre for the harm he had done.

This became one of the first missions to be turned over to the Mexican government. General Mariano Vallejo was the leader who took over. He took many herds of animals and rich land for himself. This was land that by new law should have belonged to the Indians of the Mission.

TODAY AT THE MISSION

The weather crumbled and washed the buildings away. Now nothing is left of the old Mission. A new church stands on the land which is today the town of San Rafael.

24

SAN FRANCISCO SOLANO

Twenty-first Mission, founded July 4, 1823

Russian fur trappers lived in the far North. They built a fort called Fort Ross at Bodega Bay. The Mexican government was against this. They wanted to stop Russia from taking over California. For this reason the last Mission was founded close by. It is the only one to be built after Mexican Independence.

Father Jose Altimira wanted a mission of his own to run. He did not like his life at Mission Dolores. What could he do? He had been a priest only a few years. No one would listen to him. Then he came up with an idea.

He visited his friend Governor Don Luis Arguello in Monterey. "Why not close Missions Dolores and San Rafael?" he suggested. "We could open a new mission in Sonoma to keep out the Russians who might take over the land. He liked Father Altimira's plan.

The governor gave his permission. Father Altimira set out on his journey with a group of soldiers to find a place. He came to a beautiful valley the Indians called The Valley of the Moon. It was here the young padre chose to found the Mission.

Father Senan who was President of the Missions then became angry. Who did Altimira think he was? Only the President of the Missions could decide to build a mission. Other priests were angry too. There was much quarreling about it. It was finally decided that Missions Dolores and San Rafael and the new San Francisco Solano Mission would stay open.

Older missions usually gave animals and supplies to a new mission. Not much was given to this one because of hard feelings. Surprisingly, the Russians at Fort Ross gave them a small number of cattle.

Most of the adobe buildings were built the first year and a half. Everything was going well, though the padre complained. He thought the other padres were against the Mission. He was sure they discouraged Indians from coming here. Father Altimira was wrong. Many Indians did come. They came from San Rafael, Dolores, and San Jose Missions.

Few Indians wanted to stay. The priest caused trouble. He could have used kindness and love to teach them about religion and mission life. Instead, he punished them often.

The Indians became so unhappy that they attacked the Mission and set fire to buildings. Afterwards, many Indians went back to their old missions. Some went to live in the mountains. The unhappy priest left too. He roamed from one mission to another, never staying long at any. Finally, he went back to Spain.

Another padre came to the Mission. Father Buenaventura Fortuni was a good man who was friendly and kind. Many Indians came back to live at the Mission. They were happy here for a short time longer.

Then General Mariano Vallejo took over the Mission. He divided the land among the Indians. Many turned it back to him in return for their care. The padres had made them too dependent on the mission system. With the padres gone, no one was left to look out for them.

Through the years, the Mission was used for many things. It became a blacksmith shop and later a saloon. It was also used as a barn for animals and a storeroom for hay.

TODAY AT THE MISSION

This Mission is one of the two owned by the State of California. It is now called Sonoma Mission State Historic Park. There is a museum to see. The chapel built by Vallejo and the priests' house are left. Vallejo's own house is nearby.

Beautiful watercolor paintings by Chris Jorgensen hang inside the Mission. He traveled up the coast of California visiting the missions in the early days by wagon. He studied and painted them for many years.

25
ASISTENCIAS: THE LITTLE MISSIONS

(Besides the missions, there were also asistencias. An *asistencia* was a branch mission belonging to a larger "mother" mission. In early California, some asistencias were only chapels. Other asistencias were like small missions with buildings for the padre and Indians to live, workrooms, and storerooms. Sometimes the padre lived there all the time. Other times he would travel from the larger mission to give church services.

Why were they needed? The missions were built along the coast of California. Many Indians lived in the mountains or far from the ocean. The padres wanted to teach them about Christianity too.)

Padre Payeras who was President of the Missions at one time had a plan. Why not build a second group of missions? They could be built near where these Indians lived. The governor turned the plan down. Over many years, these smaller asistencias were built. It was hoped by the padres that one day they would become full missions.

One of the most important asistencias was San Antonio de Pala. The story of this asistencia began when Father Juan Mariner came looking for land. He wanted to find a good spot for a new mission. In August, 1795, he came to the Pala Valley. He liked the beautiful land and the river flowing through it. The bright, friendly Indians welcomed him. He wanted the San Luis Rey de Francia Mission to be built here. Others wanted it to be built closer to the ocean. When it was, this land was forgotten for a while.

Father Peyri was the padre at Mission San Luis Rey. He wanted to interest the Indians of this valley in Christianity. He invited them to come live at the Mission. They liked living in their beautiful valley and did not want to leave it. Still, they seemed interested in the new religion.

The padre decided it was time to do something about it. Taking another padre and a group of Mission Indians, he walked twenty miles up the river to the Pala Valley. There he chose the land for the asistencia on June 13, 1816. It was founded as a branch of Mission San Luis Rey.

It took several years to build the buildings. The padre showed the Indians how to make thousands of adobe bricks and tiles. They cut down cedar trees growing nearby for roof beams. With horses and oxen, they carried them to the Mission.

They built a chapel long and narrow. Inside they laid tiles for the floor and painted the walls. A bell tower was built apart from the other buildings. Rocks from the river were used for a base. Most of the tower was made out of adobe bricks fifty feet tall. Two bells were hung in it.

There are two stories told about it. One is of a bird that landed on the cross as Father Peyri put it on top of the tower. The bird was so happy it started to sing and dropped a cactus seed from its mouth. The seed sprouted and a cactus grew.

The other story is about Father Peyri climbing the tower. He put a cactus at the foot of the cross. It was to be a symbol of religion coming to the wild lands.

Bell tower at Pala

The Indians worked hard and built a water channel from tiles. When they were through with the buildings, it looked like a small mission. They were built in a square. There were rooms for the padres and Indians, storehouses, a granary, and fences for the animals.

Fewer Indians came here than that of major missions. Still, there were herds of animals. The Indians planted crops of wheat, corn, beans, and other plants to eat. Most of the grain for the larger Mission was grown here. They had a vineyard for grapes and orchards with fruit and olive trees growing. Soon more Indians came. After a few years, there were over a thousand Indians.

Why were so many Indians interested in the new religion? Their own religion was like the Christian religion in some ways. The Indians believed in one god. Their name for him was Cinigchinich. He showed them how to live their daily lives. They believed in a future life after death. There were many ceremonies in this religion too. They liked the new ceremonies of the Christian padres. For some of

these reasons, they accepted Christianity easier than some
of the other California tribes.

The asistencia went well until secularization came in
1834. This meant the Mexican government replaced the padres
with administrators to run the missions. Mission San Luis
Rey had trouble. Government leaders had their eyes on the
fine land. During those days, Pala was the church center of
the valley for several smaller chapels built for ranches
nearby. Trouble came later to them.

For this reason, the statue of San Luis Rey from the
Mission church was sent here. The Indians buried it for
safety. Then they dug it up and put it in their own chapel.
A story is told about it. One day two men tried to steal
it. They tried to move it closer to the door. As they did,
the statue became heavier. It was so heavy they could not
drag it out the door. One of them shot his gun at it,
hitting one of the arms. Still, it could not be moved.
They tried carrying it back to where it belonged. As they
did, it became lighter. The two thieves were afraid and ran
out the door.

On August 22, 1835, Mission San Luis Rey and this
asistencia were taken over by Pio Pico and Pablo de la
Portilla. Pico ran it badly, and the Indians suffered.
After Pico was fired, he would not give back the land. He
sold it to Antonio J. Cot and Jose A. Pico on May 18, 1846.
They paid $2,000 in silver and $437.50 in wheat. The sale
was against the law.

Missionary padres did not live here after this. They
still did come once in a while to hold church services.

TODAY AT THE ASISTENCIA

San Antonio de Pala looks much like it did in the early
days. Buildings have been rebuilt. Bells in the bell tower
are still rung to call the Indians to church. This is the
only church in the mission chain still used for services by
the Indians. The bell tower is famous.

The museum has many interesting objects. There are
woven baskets and pottery made by the Indians. Several
statues can be seen. The statue of San Luis Rey is here.
It and the one of Mother Mary were made by Mexican artists.
Statues of St. Anthony and St. Dominc are by Indian artists.

There is an Indian reservation nearby of Palatingua Indians. These are a different tribe from the Shoshonean Indians of mission days. Each year the Corpus Christi Fiesta is given. It is a celebration of God's love for man. Since 1816, not one year has been missed in celebrating this fiesta.

Because of the interest in this asistencia over the years, it has now become a full mission. Many do not count it among the list of missions since it became one after mission days.

OTHER ASISTENCIAS

Many of the asistencias have been destroyed. In the early days they were built as they were needed. Among them were Santa Ysabel, San Bernardino, Santa Margarita, Las Flores Nuestra Senora La Reina de Los Angeles, San Miguel, San Miguelito, Mesa Grande, and Santa Ysabel.

26

THE END OF THE MISSIONS

"War! War!" cried the messenger. "Mexico is at war!"
News came that Mexico had declared their independence
from Spain. They wanted to rule themselves. They grew
tired of the King of Spain telling them what to do. The
battle called the Hildago Revolt broke out in 1810. Suddenly, all supplies were cut off to the missions. During the
war, they could not trade with other countries or Mexico for
what they needed. The government ordered the missions to
support the soldiers and their families. The government no
longer had money to pay the soldiers.

More shoes, more blankets, and more food. The demands
of the soldiers never ended. They would not work. The
mission would have to take care of them. The padres wrote
letters to the government. They told how unfair this was to
the Indians and the missions. Their letters did not do any
good.

There had always been trouble with the soldiers. Not
many people at first wanted to come to California from

Mexico. Some of them had been criminals back in Mexico. These people came to guard and protect the missions. They fought with the Indians. Often they argued with the padres and would not do what the padres ordered.

For years the missions went on like this. The heavy load of supporting the soldiers discouraged the Indians. Soon supplies disappeared and people went hungry. Life was very difficult for the Indians.

"Mexico has won the war!" was the excited cry. Mexico won their independence from Spain in 1821. This was not good news to the missions. Things did not get any better. They became worse. Leaders in the Mexican government looked at the rich lands of the missions with greedy thoughts. They wanted to get rid of the padres and missions. They wanted to take the land. They passed many laws to make this come true.

They made the padres sign a paper called "an oath of loyalty." It said they would obey the new Mexican government. The padres were Spanish citizens. They felt loyal to Spain and would not sign the paper. The leaders became angry. They passed another law to make Spaniards under the age of 60 leave the country. This meant most of the padres were forced to leave.

The Indians became Mexican citizens. They could vote now, but few were given the chance. Many were tired of the strict mission life. In later years they enjoyed little freedom. Many ran away, but now even more left.

Mexican leaders came to rule the missions after the padres left. The land belonged to the Indians. It was supposed to be divided among them. Settlers and leaders took most of it instead. Governor Pio Pico sold many of the missions, though it was against the law.

What was left for the Indians? The Spaniards had come and taken their land and changed their lives. Few Indians had been taught to read and write. They had spent their time working at useful trades for the good of the missions. They did not have much practice in governing themselves. The padres had made them too dependent. Many knew no other life than mission life. What did they know of living off

the land? Their people had left that life many years before. But some did try to go back to the mountains and live
in the old ways. Others went to work on newly-formed
ranchos or stayed on at missions until they were forced to
leave.

The mission system that had begun in 1769, ended about
70 years later. It had lasted about as long as one person's
lifetime. In that time, it had changed the lives of the
Indians forever.)

27
FATHER JUNIPERO SERRA

Founder of the Missions

On November 21, 1713, Miguel Jose Serra was born. He grew up in the small village of Petra on the island of Majorca in Spain.

His parents were named Antonio and Margarita. They were poor people who worked hard but could not read or write. But in their home, there was much love and kindness for Miguel and his sister, Juana.

As a boy, Miguel was shy and sickly. Sometimes he was not strong enough to play with the other children. His life became centered around the Catholic church. His faith in God was strong. He sang in the choir and learned his lessons well.

As he grew older, Miguel decided to become a Franciscan priest. At first the school turned him down. Those who knew him told them what a good priest Miguel would make.

When he became a priest, he changed his name to Junipero Serra. At the same time, he also became a teacher. He taught classes at the University of Majorca for seven years. The students liked him, and he could have spent the rest of his life teaching. But he had a dream. He wanted to become a missionary. A missionary is a religious person who wants to travel to other countries and tell those people about God. Then he heard missionaries were needed in Mexico. He told them he would go. First he was sent to San Fernando College to a school for missionaries. After this, he was put in charge of five missions that were already built. He went to live in the Sierra Gorda Mountains of Central Mexico. Here he worked for nine years teaching the Indians Christianity. These were happy years for Father Serra.

Next, the church wanted him to become a traveling missionary. He was to preach all over Mexico wherever he was needed. He did this for eight years. Sometimes it was very dangerous. His travels took him to mining camps and seaports. They took him along jungle rivers where deadly snakes hung from trees over his head. Often he spent the night where fierce, wild animals roamed. But Father Serra was a brave man.

The church leader knew this. When there were missions to be established in California, Father Serra was chosen to be President. He was 55 years old by then. Bravely, he set out to found the first nine of twenty-one missions.

Believing strongly in the mission system, he walked many miles by foot to establish new missions. He traveled to check on old ones. His many journeys caused him to limp. Often when he was sick, he would still travel anyway. Finally on August 28, 1784, he died of a sickness called tuberculosis. He was seventy-one years old. He had served his church as a missionary for thirty-five years.

CALIFORNIA MISSIONS AND THEIR LOCATIONS

San Diego de Alcala

    Mission Valley, off Interstate 8

San Carlos Borromeo de Carmelo

    3080 Rio Road in Carmel

San Antonio de Padua

    About five miles west of Jolon

San Gabriel Arcangel

    537 West Mission Drive, San Gabriel

San Luis Obispo de Tolosa

    San Luis Obispo, Monterey & Chorro

San Francisco de Asis

    16th and Dolores Street in San Francisco

San Juan Capistrano

    Off Highway 5, in the town of San Juan Capistrano

Santa Clara de Asis

    Santa Clara on University of Santa Clara campus

San Buenaventura

    Main Street in Ventura, off Highway 101

Santa Barbara

    2201 Laguna Street in the resort town of Santa Barbara

La Purisima Concepcion

    Northeast of Lompoc, west of Bullton on State Highway 246

Santa Cruz

    In Santa Cruz on the corner of Emmet & High Streets

Nuestra Senora de la Soledad

    A few miles from the town of Soledad on Ft. Romie Road

San Jose de Guadalupe

    In Fremont at Highway 238 and Washington Blvd.

San Juan Bautista

    San Juan Bautista, off State Highway 156

San Miguel Arcangel

    North of Paso Robles off Highway 101

San Fernando Rey de Espana

    15151 San Fernando Mission Blvd., San Fernando

San Luis Rey de Francia

    East of the town of Oceanside on State Highway 76

Santa Ines

    1760 Mission Drive, Solvang, just east of Buellton

San Rafael Arcangel

    Fifth Avenue & Court Street in the City of San Rafael

San Francisco Solano

    In the main part of the town of Sonoma

BIBLIOGRAPHY

BOOKS

Ainsworth, Katherine and Edward. *In the Shade of the Juniper Tree: A Life of Fray Junipero Serra*, Doubleday, 1970.

Bauer, Helen. *California Indian Days*, Doubleday, 1968.

Bauer, Helen. *California Mission Days*, Doubleday, 1951.

Bleeker, Sonia. *The Mission Indians of California*, William Morrow & Co., 1956.

Brown, Karl F. *California Missions: a Guide to the Historic Trails of the Padres*, Garden City Publishing Co., Inc., 1939.

Carillo, J. M. *The Story of Mission San Antonio de Pala*, Paisano Press, 1959.

Englehardt, Fray Zephryrin. *Mission Nuestra Senora de la Soledad*, Mission Santa Barbara, 1929.

--- *Mission San Carlos Borromeo (Carmelo)*, Mission Santa Barbara, 1934.

---*Mission San Juan Bautista*, Mission Santa Barbara, 1931.

---*Mission San Luis Obispo*, Mission Santa Barbara, 1933.

---*Mission Santa Ines*, Mission Santa Barbara, 1932.

---*San Antonio de Padua*, Ballena Press, 1929.

---*San Buenaventura*, Mission Santa Barbara, 1930.

---*San Diego Mission*, The James Barry Co., 1920.

---*San Fernando Rey*, Franciscan Herald Press, 1927.

---*San Francisco or Mission Dolores*, Franciscan Herald Press, 1924.

---*San Gabriel Mission and the Beginning of Los Angeles*, Mission San Gabriel, 1927.

Engelhardt, Fray Zephyrin. *San Juan Capistrano Mission*, The Standard Printing Co., 1922.

---*San Luis Rey Mission*, The James Barry Co., 1921.

---*San Miguel Arcangel*, Mission Santa Barbara, 1929.

---*Santa Barbara Mission*, The James Barry Co., 1923.

Foster, Lee. *The Beautiful California Missions*, Beautiful America Publishing Co., 1977.

Goodman, Marian. *Missions of California*, Redwood City Tribune, 1962.

Hawthorne, Hildegarde. *California's Missions--Their Romance and Beauty*, Appleton-Century Co., Inc., 1942.

Hoover, Mildred Brooke and Rensch, H. E. and E. G.; revised by Teiser, Ruth. *Historic Spots in California*, Stanford University Press, 1948.

James, George Wharton. *In and Out of the Old Missions of California*, Little, Brown & Co., 1905.

Kocher, Paul. *California's Old Missions: The Story of the Founding of the 21 Franciscan Missions in Spanish Alta California 1769-1823*, Franciscan Herald Press, 1976.

Older, Mrs. Fremont. *California Missions and Their Romances*, Tudor Publishing Co., 1945.

Roberts, Helen M. *Mission Tales*, Pacific Books, Publishers, 1948.

Smilie, Robert S. *The Sonoma Mission: San Francisco Solano de Sonoma*, Valley Publishers, 1975.

Sunset. *The California Missions: a Pictorial History*, Lane Book Co., 1974.

Tompkins, Walker A. *Old Spanish Santa Barbara*, McNally and Loftin Publishers, 1967.

Torchiana, H. V. Van Coenen. *Story of the Mission Santa Cruz* Paul Elder and Co., 1933.

Ziebold, Edna B. *Indians of Early Southern California*, Perc B. Sapsis Publisher, 1969.

BIBLIOGRAPHY

PAMPHLETS

Earnest, Aileen Ryan. "Mission Vestments," 1975.

Engbeck, Joseph H., Jr. "La Purisima Mission State Historic Park," State of California.

Geiger, Maynard. "Father Junipero Serra Paintings," Fransican Fathers, 1958.

---"The Indians of Mission Santa Barbara in Paganism and Christianity," Franciscan Fathers, 1960.

Gordon, Dudley. "Junipero Serra: California's First Citizen," Cultural Assets Press, 1969.

Guilfoyle, Rev. Merlin J. "Dolores or Mission San Francisco."

Harrington, Marie. "Mission San Fernando: a Guide," San Fernando Valley Historical Society, Inc., 1971.

Iversen, Eva C. "California's Mission San Miguel Arcangel," published by Franiscan Padres.

Kochner, Paul H. "Mission San Luis Obispo de Tolosa; a Historical Sketch," Blake Printing & Publishing, 1972.

Lowman, Hubert A. "California's Mission San Luis Rey," Franciscan Padres.

McIntyre, Francis A. "Padre Junipero Serra and the California Missions," 1949.

Merrill, King. "Old Mission Santa Ines," Viking Press, King Merrill Associates.

Morrison, Col. E. G. Morie. "Sonoma, California's Mission San Francisco Solano," Mission Sesquicentennial Commission, 1973.

Mylar, Isacc L. "Early Days at the Mission San Juan Bautista," Valley Publishers, 1976.

Ray, Sister Mary Dominic and Engbeck, Joseph H., Jr. "Gloria Dei: The Story of California Mission Music," State of California.

Serra, J. "San Diego de Alcala: California's First Mission."

Tac, Pablo; edited and translated by Hewes, Gordon and Minna. "Indian Life at Mission San Luis Rey: A Record of California Mission Life," Old Mission, 1958.

GLOSSARY

adobe- sun-dried bricks made of clay earth, straw, and water
alcalde- Indian leader elected by his people at the mission
altar- a table used by religious people in church services
arrowhead- the pointed tip of an arrow made of stone or metal
asistencia- small mission or sub-mission
baptism- religious ceremony given for a person to become a
  Christian
blacksmith- a person who makes objects out of iron
carpenter- a person who makes objects out of wood
ceremony- ritual
chapel- small church
community- a group of people living in the same area
convent- a church and building for religious women to live
design- drawing
dialects- different ways of saying the same language
earthquake- a shaking of the earth
establish- *See* settle
expedition- a group of people taking a long trip to a faraway
  place
fiesta- a party
frijolera- Spanish word for cannon
governor- a leader who rules a country or territory
kiln- a brick oven used to bake adobe bricks
loom- a machine used to weave cloth
medicine man or woman- a person thought to be able to heal the
  sick and talk to the gods
miracle- an event that cannot be explained
missionary- religious person who wants to travel to other
  countries to tell people about God
padre- Spanish name for priest *See* priest
planks- wood boards
pozole- a stew of vegetables and beef
presidio- fort
priest- a religious person in some churches
pueblo- town
regiodore- Indian leader elected to help the alcalde
saint- a person who is considered holy by the church
saloon- a bar
sandstone- yellow stone used to build some of mission churches
settle- to come to live
shield- an object designed to protect a person
siesta- Spanish word for rest
stable- a building where horses are kept
tallow- animal fat; used to make soap and candles
tanner- a person who tans animal hides
tattoo- to mark or decorate the skin
territory- land

tile- piece of clay baked in kiln, often used for roofs

trade- exchanging one object for another or a type of skilled
  work

tribe- a group of people who share the same language and culture

vat- pit

viceroy- a leader who rules a country for the king

village- a small group of houses

water channel- a system of water pipes

INDEX

ABOUT THE AUTHOR

Linda Lyngheim has been a librarian for the Glendale Public Library for nine years. She is a California history enthusiast and received her Bachelor of Arts degree in the social sciences from California State University, Fresno. Her Masters degree is in library science from the University of Southern California. As an author, she has written an adult book, *Bee Pollen: Nature's Miracle Health Food*, published by Wilshire Book Company, 1979. She has written magazine articles for *School Library Journal* on children's literature including: "Taking Laughter Seriously," March, 1981 and "Hanging Tough," November, 1981. She is a past book reviewer for *SLJ*. Currently, she has just completed two adult pamphlets for Langtry Publications: "The Rancho Era of California," and "California Historical Novels" (an annotated bibliography). She resides in Los Angeles with her husband.

ABOUT THE ILLUSTRATOR

Phyllis Garber is a graduate of Carnegie Mellon University. She studied at Pittsburgh Art Institute and Pasadena School of Art and with Robert Uecker, Patricia Short, Jean Freeman, and David Whelan. She has exhibited in juried shows by the Costa Mesa Art Association and the Laguna Niguel Art Association. She has received many local art awards for her watercolors.

ORDER FORM

For additional books or pamphlets on California history, please send the following:

QUANTITY	BOOKS OR PAMPHLETS	PRICE
_____	*The Indians and the California Missions* (book) by Linda Lyngheim	$ 9.95 each
_____	"The California Rancho Era" (adult pamphlet) by Linda Lyngheim	$ 4.00 each
_____	"The California Novel: An Annotated Bibliography" (adult pamphlet) by Linda Lyngheim	$ 3.50 each

Subtotal $_____

California Residents Add 6 1/2% sales tax $_____

Postage and handling:
books: $1.50 for first book, $.50 for each additional copy. $_____
Pamphlets: $.50 postage each   TOTAL $_____

SHIP TO (Please Print or Type)
Name _____
Organization _____
Address _____
City, State, Zip _____

BILL TO (Please Print or Type)
Name _____
Organization _____
Address _____
City, State, Zip _____

PAYMENT

_____ CHECK OR MONEY ORDER ENCLOSED

_____ PLEASE BILL ME (Libraries, schools, and bookstores ONLY)

Please make check payable or mail purchase order to:

LANGTRY PUBLICATIONS
7838 Burnet Avenue
Van Nuys, CA 91405-1051

Allow 4 weeks for delivery